D0859736

By Joan Walsh Anglund

The Circle of the Spirit

Dearest Christine,
To a wonderful
vital woman on her
birthday. Remain
young in spirit.
Love you always,
Amy
'86

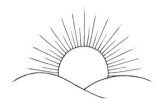

The Circle of the Spirit

by

Joan Walsh Anglund

Random House New York

Library of Congress Cataloging in Publication Data

Anglund, Joan Walsh.
The circle of the spirit.
I. Title.
PS3551.N47C5 1983   811'.54   82-20460
ISBN 0-394-53080-2
Manufactured in the United States of America

4 6 8 9 7 5 3

For my
Dear Nana,
Abbie Pfeifer

The Angels came
        . . . and there was loveliness.
I did not ask
       . . . and yet I heard,
and the voice was music,
      and all things turned
           wondrous
      at its sound
  . . . and Peace was
         Everywhere.

I have come
> to tell you
>> of the Way,

And the Way
> is
>> the Circle

And the Circle
> is
>> the Source

And the Source
> is
>> Life

And Life
> is
>> the Light.

Therefore,
> those of the Circle
>> shall drink of the Source
>> and become as the Light
>>> that lives
>>>> and nourishes.

There is no Question
  and there is no Answer
that is not
   contained
    within the Circle.
Therefore,
  do not ask Why
. . . for the Circle knows,
  and
   because you are
    of the Circle
So do you, also, know
   . . . and yet
    do not know
     of your knowing.
But the Circle shall turn . . .
  and, in its turning
  all Truth
   shall be made apparent.

The Circle
        has no beginning
The Circle
        has no ending
The Circle is . . .
                and continues,
                        . unendingly
        . . . beyond the Circle
                of our understanding.

The Circle is.
                The Circle is complete,
and in the Circle
        all parts are equal.
The Circle turns
        . . . revealing first this side,
                then the next.
        Thus, there seems to be Change.

But the Circle *is*
                . . . at all times
                . . . on all sides,
                        and does not change,
                                but
                                        is.

We see but part
            of the Circle,
    and this
            is the illusion
                    of Time.

But Time
        is only the Light
                    falling upon the Circle
        illuminating a part here
                    . . . or there,
            of what continues
                    and is,
            so that we may see it more clearly

                    . . . and thereby understand.

All parts
        are necessary
                to the Circle.

All parts
        are equal
                to the Circle.

Life is a Circle.
  If a leaf falls
            does it not grow again
           . . . in the Circle
                  . . . of another Season?
If a man dies,
          does he not live again
           . . . in the Circle
                  . . . of another Age?

The Waters teach us,
        the Sands teach us
. . . the Winds speak
            . . . the Grasses murmur
                        . . . of the Truth
        . . . but
            who
                will listen?

We are Eyes
            . . . meant to see,
We are Ears
            . . . meant to hear

        . . . but
            the World distracts,
                while the Way
                        lies ahead
        . . . waiting,
                for us.

The Word
         has been Spoken,
  why need we speak it
                   again?
Because
       the path that is worn
                      by many feet
          will be followed
                      by many others,
      and the Way
                is made apparent
                by the pathway
                          worn
                          by its followers.

Do not desire the Way,
      for the Way
                is yours
                     . . . without desire.

Do not search for the Way,
      for the Way
                finds you
                     . . . without your searching.

The butterfly hovers,
      and finds the flower.

The flower waits
            . . . knowing
                  the butterfly
                        will come.

Why fear Death?
                . . . it is nothing.

  It is a thin curtain
                . . . less than gauze,
                                between us.
For the Spirit
                is the same
    on both sides.
          And we are One
                . . . in Death
                                as well as Life.

There is no Age . . .
          There is no Time . . .
                There is no Death . . .

          In the Circle
                of the Spirit
                . . . there is only Light
                                . . . and Life
                                        . . . and Love!

We are as a closed eye
                . . . that will not see.
    a clasped ear
                . . . that will not hear,
    a clenched fist
                . . . that will not open,
        a clamped jaw
                . . . that will not unlock.

How then,
        can the Spirit
                        enter us
        . . . and give us
                        nourishment?

Only the open gate
                    can receive
                                visitors.
    Only the open hand
                        can receive
                                    gifts.
    Only the open mind
                        can receive
                                    wisdom.
    Only the open heart
                        can receive
                                    love.

31

Within
      our letting go
is the seed
      of our receiving.

For to find
      the Truth,
one must lose
      the Self.

Do not ask
        . . . but listen.
  For the Angels sing . . .
        but
            not at *our* command.

We ask not for the Sun
        . . . and yet,
            it warms us.
We ask not for the Moon
        . . . and yet,
            it lights our way.
  Therefore,
        do not ask
            . . . but receive,
  and the receiving
        shall be
            your prayer.

Within the spinning of events
. . . which is Time,
is the still center
. . . which is Truth.

. . . Until we reach that center
we are but a swirling whirlpool
. . . with no purpose.

37

The candle does not know
      . . . and yet its flame
                  is steady.

Be thou also
   as the candle flame
           . . . unknowing
           . . . and yet constant.

For tomorrow
      . . . you shall know.
But today,
    you must trust.

The Spirit is still.
  It does not fly here or there
      . . . as leaves in the Autumn,
                         without direction.
The Spirit stays
         . . . and understands.
If there is a mountain,
     need we climb it
         to know that it is there?
We need not partake of all things
    to know them.
They are ours
    . . . without our touching them
           or tasting of their flesh.
  For the Spirit does not grasp or eat to live.
  It perceives,
    and by perceiving . . . surrounds
         . . . as the Circle surrounds.
And by enclosing
    . . . understands,
      and unites.
For to understand,
     is to become One
      with that which is understood.

Release
     . . . and you will receive.
Openness
        invites.
  It is a waiting space
           asking to be filled.
When the mind is closed
        the Spirit is locked without.
    It cannot enter.
        It cannot nourish.

The Spirit is as the Wind
           that blows . . .
  It is as the River
        . . . that flows . . .
It cannot be held
     it must be free . . .
Only Openness
      can contain the Spirit
     as it passes into . . .
           through . . .
           and beyond.

The Spirit is not of the Flesh
    for the Flesh is Heavy
                and the Spirit is of the Light.
Thus does it move as the Light
    that cannot be caught by the hand
      or touched,
          and therefore defiled.

For the Spirit is free
      . . . and flies above and away
              from the Flesh.
For those who live in the Spirit
            . . . the Flesh retreats,
      and the appetites thereof, wither,
        and have no strength.

For the Flesh shall die
    . . . but the Spirit shall live
           . . . and endure forever.
    Be, therefore, of the Spirit
        . . . of the Light
            . . . of the Circle
          . . . that continues
            without end.

One tree
       holds
           a hundred birds.
Yet,
   the birds fly away,
      and the tree remains
               . . . and endures.

Be as the tree
   . . . rooted
     in
     the
     Earth
        . . . yet
           touching
           the
           Sky.

Shadows . . .
    Doubt is a Shadow
       . . . like a dark bird wing
              across your bright Belief.
    Let its shadow pass . . .
       Do not follow its flickering darkness
            to where its deeper shadows nest.

Death can seem the Darkest Shadow.
    . . . But it is only that . . . a Shadow.
            Be not afraid,
  It has no substance
        . . . and passes,
             as a Shadow,
  only a shadow,
       a momentary darkness
          . . . upon a glistening
               terrain.

Because
     the sun dips
          its bright face
               beneath the horizon,
Do we doubt
          that we shall find it again,
               tomorrow
          . . . shining as brightly?

So, too,
     though the Spirit
          dims its Light
        in that which we have named Death
     Shall we not again discover
          that same bright force
        waiting for us
          beyond this passing Shadow?

Though the eye
          does not see
The Soul
     knows
        the Way.

        . . . Trust.

Holding hands
        we are a Circle
                    . . . of the Spirit.
    It is not accidental
        that we have come
                to be together here
        for we have joined before.

The Spirit is the Unseen Circle
    within
        the Circle of the Senses.

Trust
    the Unseen.
        . . . for Life itself
            is unseen.

It dwells
    in temporary homes,
  but moves on,
      beyond the shapes
        which contain it
          for their instant.

The Spirit that speaks through you
    is as the Light
             that shines
                        through the Lamp.

    The Lamp does not create it
        The Lamp is but the Vessel
                    which holds the Light.

    But the Light is a force
                    moving through the Lamp
        and out
              to those who would see
          . . . illuminating their way.

The Way waits
         . . . and we must walk it
  we each
       must take the Journey
               to the Truth

If we do not begin today
            . . . we must begin
                   tomorrow.

This body
    we wear
is but
   the clothing
      of the Spirit
to be discarded
     when no longer needed.

We live *in* the Body
. . . but we are not *of* the Body.

We dwell *in* the Flesh
. . . but we are not *of* the Flesh.

The Flesh is not our Home
Our Home is in the Light.

And the Spirit *is* the Light
and the Light *is* the Spirit
and the Spirit is
of
God.

JOAN WALSH ANGLUND, the much-loved author-artist of such celebrated titles as *A Friend Is Someone Who Likes You* and *Love Is a Special Way of Feeling*, lives with her family in an eighteenth-century house in Connecticut. Her books, whose sales number in the millions, have been widely published, and include editions in England, Germany, Sweden, Denmark, Norway, Spain, Brazil and South Africa.